Make a Friend, Be a Friend

Eric Braun

Illustrated by Steve Mark

free spirit
PUBLISHING®

Library of Congress Cataloging-in-Publication Data
Names: Braun, Eric, 1971– author. | Mark, Steve, illustrator.
Title: Make a friend, be a friend / Eric Braun ; illustrated by Steve Mark.
Description: Minneapolis : Free Spirit Publishing Inc., 2021. | Series: Little laugh & learn
    | Audience: Ages 6–9
Identifiers: LCCN 2020053190 (print) | LCCN 2020053191 (ebook) | ISBN 9781631986291
    (paperback) | ISBN 9781631986307 (pdf) | ISBN 9781631986314 (epub)
Subjects: LCSH: Friendship—Juvenile literature.
Classification: LCC BF575.F66 B736 2021 (print) | LCC BF575.F66 (ebook)
    | DDC 177/.62—dc23
LC record available at https://lccn.loc.gov/2020053190
LC ebook record available at https://lccn.loc.gov/2020053191

Free Spirit Publishing does not have control over or assume responsibility for author or
third-party websites and their content.

Reading Level Grade 2; Interest Level Ages 6–9
Fountas & Pinnell Guided Reading Level M

Edited by Marjorie Lisovskis
Cover and interior design by Emily Dyer

10 9 8 7 6 5 4 3 2
Printed in USA
R18860122

Free Spirit Publishing Inc.
6325 Sandburg Road, Suite 100
Minneapolis, MN 55427-3674
(612) 338-2068
help4kids@freespirit.com
freespirit.com

Acknowledgments

A big high-five and thanks to Margie Lisovskis, friend and editor, for her invaluable vision and support, and for knowing when to pull me back from one too many gross jokes; as well as to Judy Galbraith and everyone at Free Spirit Publishing for their dedication to supporting kids.

CONTENTS

CHAPTER 1

Fantastic Facts About Friends

It's great to have a friend!

Friends make good times better. They make bad times better too.

Friends do fun things together.

They share jokes.

They share their fears and the things that make them sad.

If your feet stink, friends don't plug their nose and run away.

(Okay, maybe they do. But then they come back.)

Friends stand by each other when times are tough. They stand UP for each other too.

They learn from each other.

Sometimes friends disagree or fight. When that happens, they talk and work it out.

What's great about friends?

Friends are there for you and care for you.

They share with you and dare with you.

They can be your caring, sharing, daring partners in life. How's that for fantastic?

Some kids have lots of friends. Others have a few. Either way is great! Read on to find ways to make friends and be a better friend, so you and your friends can stick together. If you and a friend are fighting or having a disagreement, you can learn how to fix things.

That way YOU can be a fantastic friend finder. And a powerful pal.

CHAPTER 2

Hi There! How to Find and Make Friends

Sometimes new friends are right in front of you. **Hello!**

Your next friend might sit by you in school or live near you. A friend might be in the same after-school group as you.

If you want another way to find friends, you could join a new activity. Try an art club or a sport you like.

9

You can tell that someone might be a good friend for you if they seem nice. Or if they laugh at the same things as you. (Maybe you both think baboons are hilarious.) Or if they love sardine smoothies just as much as you do.

Meet and Greet

If you want to get to know someone, you can **greet** them. Say:

- "Hi!"
- "Hey!"
- "Hello."
- "Yo."
- "What's up?"
- "How's it going?"

A greeting is often enough to get started.

Take your time. At first, it's just about **connecting**. Don't invite someone for a sleepover right after you say hi for the first time.

Start a Conversation

The next step is to talk with the person more. A good way to start is by asking about something you're both interested in. If you see them playing something you like, you can say, "Hey, I like that game too. Do you want to see some of my cards?"

Here are some other ideas for getting a **conversation** started:

- "What's your favorite book?"

- "What do you like to watch?"

- "What do you listen to?"

- "What games do you like?"

- "Who do you live with?"

- "What does your family do for fun?"

It can be nice to give a compliment, but only if you really mean it.

- "I like your shoes."

- "You did great on the test."

- "Wow, nice throw!"

- "You're really good at dancing."

- "That was awesome! I've never heard anyone belch that loud."

BURP

15

WHAT WOULD YOU DO?
A Story Starring You

It takes time to learn how to make friends. Here's a story to help you practice.

Once there was a smart, charming young person. That's right, this person was you!

Imagine . . .

You are going to join a new after-school group. You are super nervous. It's your first day. You don't know anyone there.

But you are brave! (Of course you are—you're the hero of this story.) You bravely walk in. You bravely meet the other kids.

You meet one boy who says it is also his first day.

You meet a girl who is wearing a t-shirt with your favorite character, Super Puppy.

Another kid smiles at you and tells a funny story.

Later, the group leader says it's time for a break. All the kids are just hanging around. Now is your chance to talk with someone.

How do you want the story to go from here? Who could you talk to? How could you start the conversation?

CHAPTER 3

Four Ways to Show You Want to Be a Friend

Making friends is like eating a gigantic banana sandwich. No, that doesn't mean it's weirdly delicious. It means it's a two-person job!

HEE HEE

20

Have you found someone who seems like they would be a good friend? Terrific! Now your job is to show them that **you** would be a good friend to **them**. Here are four ways to do it:

- Be kind.

- Share.

- Be a good sport.

- Start a friendly chat.

HA
HA
HA

1. Be Kind

This might be obvious. But good friends are kind.

Be polite. Say please and thank you. Don't cut in line. And never steal anyone's dessert. (Even if it's your favorite.)

Think about people's feelings—not just your own!

Don't make mean jokes about others, even if you think it's just kidding.

2. Share

You can Share games, school supplies, or jokes.

You can share good times. Invite others to play your game or join your lunch table.

And you can share your dessert. (Even if it's your favorite.)

3. Be a Good Sport

Sometimes it seems like the whole point of sports and games is to win. Maybe you know people who play like that. They act like the world will end if they're not the star of every game. Here's a question for you:

Are they fun to play with?

Winning is not what games are all about. Sure, it's fun to **try** to win. Play your hardest. But the real point is for everyone to have fun together.

Good friends don't hog the ball.

They don't get super mad when they lose.

They don't act all boasty when they win.

They don't say other people cheated. They don't complain. And they definitely don't make fun of the way somebody else plays.

Being a good sport isn't only about sports. You can be a good sport when you lose in a board game. Or when someone else gets picked for the part you wanted in a skit. Or when it's someone else's turn to be class helper. Or when someone gets a new toy you wanted.

Good friends focus on having fun,
being fair, and including everyone.

4. Start a Friendly Chat

It's time to talk. Are you ready? Just open your lips and let 'em flap.

Kidding! There's more to good conversation than blabbing. Here are three talking tips that are FRIEND-TASTIC.

Talking Tip 1: Ask questions about the other person. This will make them feel good. It shows that you are interested in them.

- "What's your hamster's name?"
- "Where did you get that cool hat?"

Talking Tip 2: Take turns. Make sure you both get a chance to talk.

Talking Tip 3: Listen to what someone says. Don't just wait for your chance to speak.

Bonus! The ideas in this book don't just help you make friends. They also help you be a good friend. You can read more about being a good friend in the next chapter.

CHAPTER 4

Three Ways to Be a Good Friend (With a Secret Ingredient!)

Once you have a friend, it doesn't mean you can start being mean or talking only about yourself. And it doesn't mean you can start acting like a poor sport.

Good friends still do all the important things you do to *make* friends. Things like being kind, asking questions about each other, giving compliments, and sharing.

But there's more you can do to make
your friendship strong and help it grow.

1. Listen

No, REALLY listen. When your friend talks, give your full attention. Notice how your friend feels. Look at your friend and nod to show that you're interested. If you don't understand something, ask a question.

Wait, why did that happen?

When you really listen to someone, you are showing **empathy**. Empathy means understanding what another person feels. And sharing those feelings.

The ability to imagine how another person feels is the key to getting along. It's the secret ingredient to friendship.

2. Be Helpful and Supportive

Friends can help each other with schoolwork, chores, and other activities.

They can also help in other, more important ways. If your friend is feeling blue or struggling with something, sometimes all they need is a friend to listen.

But sometimes they need more. You can stick up for a friend who needs an ally.

If you don't know how to support your friend, ask.

"I'm sorry you feel bad. What can I do to help you?"

3. Try New Things

Friends don't always agree on what to do. Sometimes, being a good friend means taking turns on who chooses a game. If you're lucky, you might find a new thing you like to do!

Maybe your friend loves the show *Pizza Pirates*, but you prefer *Mad Snake Babies*. Give *Pizza Pirates* a . You can watch *Mad Snake Babies* another time.

It's also fun to **try something that is new** for both of you. This is especially true if you can't agree on what to do. Maybe you've never played tennis, but your mom has a couple rackets and a few balls. Take them outside and hit the balls around for a while. You might discover something you both love.

CHAPTER 5

When Times Get Tough

You've been a good friend. You've listened. You've been supportive. You've shared and tried new things. But that doesn't mean your friendship will always be smooth sailing.

Sometimes friends have hard times. This can be true even when you do all the right things.

Even if both friends are as nice as an unexpected day off school.

Even if both friends are as sweet as a peach popsicle.

If this has happened to you, you know the truth: It can really hurt.

If your friendship is not fantastic-o, it doesn't have to be a fiasco. (No, *fiasco* is not a kind of hot sauce. It means a big, messy disaster.)

Read on to learn how to handle a hard time between friends.

Stay Calm

The most important thing is not to freak out. If you're in a conflict with a friend, do not act mean, even if your feelings are hurt. It doesn't help to talk behind your friend's back, call them names, hit them, or hide a prickly porcupine in their desk.

Staying calm can be really hard to do. When feelings get hot, it might seem like the most natural thing in the world to yell or do something hurtful.

Do your best to hold steady! Take some deep breaths. And think before you act.

Communication Is Key

If you and your friend both stay calm, you can talk about what happened. Let your friend share their side of the story. Remember what you learned about listening (page 38). Give your friend your full attention. Then it's your turn to share your side.

Here's an important rule to remember: When it's your turn to talk, talk about your own feelings. Don't accuse the other person of anything.

DON'T say: "You told everyone about my teddy bear just to embarrass me!"

DO say: "I felt really embarrassed when you told people about my teddy bear. I trusted you to keep it a secret."

This way, you have a better chance of getting your friend to understand your side. It's easier for a friend to listen when you simply tell how you feel.

If something is bothering you, it's best to talk about it soon. If you put it off, the hurt and anger might grow stronger and stronger. Kind of like a long, slow fart. It can make you miserable. So speak up!

Apologizing

After talking with your friend, you may find out that you hurt their feelings. Maybe you said or did something they thought was mean.

Maybe what you did was an accident. Maybe it wasn't.

Either way, your friend was hurt. You can start to fix things by **apologizing**.

You can apologize for hurt you caused. Most important, you can try to make things better.

"I'm sorry I broke your T-rex. I'll ask my sister to help us fix it."

What if you are the one who was hurt?
Give your friend the chance to
apologize. If your friend seems like they
really mean it, try to forgive them.

"I'm sorry I told people about your
teddy bear. I didn't know it was a secret.
I never meant to hurt you. Besides, I
think your teddy bear is cool."

Do You Need a Break?

Sometimes it's too hard for friends to make up right away. Maybe one or both of them was hurt too much. Maybe one person wants to forgive, but the other doesn't.

When that happens, it might be time to take a break from each other.

You and your friend can agree not to hang out for a few days or weeks. Maybe you will feel better about each other after some time passes.

If the two of you are on a break, it's important to keep things fair. Don't say mean things about your friend to other people.

! Important Point!

Sometimes your friendship troubles are too hard to handle on your own. When that happens, reach out to a grown-up you trust. This might be your mom or dad, or your uncle or aunt. Or it might be your teacher, or a neighbor you know well. Tell the person what's going on. Grown-ups have had lots of friendships. They might have some ideas that will help.

Fighting with a friend can feel lonely. But you don't have to face tough times alone. Get help.

WHAT WOULD YOU DO?
A Story Starring You

It's hard when friends disagree.
This story lets you think more about
ways to handle tough times.

Welcome back to another story of
everyone's favorite hero: YOU.

Imagine . . .

There's trouble in YOU-land. Uh-oh. You
and your best friend had an argument.
She thinks you told another friend that
her breath smells like sweaty socks.

She is embarrassed and mad. And it's no wonder: Sweaty sock breath sounds pretty nasty.

But the thing is, you didn't say that. And you tell her so: "I would never say anything mean about you."

Unfortunately, your friend is sure you did say it. She's so mad, she tries to hurt you back. She says *your* breath smells like booger burgers.

It works: You are hurt. And now you're as mad as she is. You start yelling at each other. Your fists are tight. Your heart is pounding. How could your BEST FRIEND say something like that about you?

And that reminds you. She's your BEST FRIEND. You don't want to be in a fight.

How can you start to fix things? Where might your story go from here?

CHAPTER 6

Friends Make Life Better

Life is better when you have a friend.
That's true for everyone.

Even if you're strong and independent.

Even if you like to be alone most of the time.

Even if social situations make you uneasy, queasy, or sneezy.

Life is still better when you have someone to share it with. It's just the way humans are.

That doesn't mean making and being friends is a snap. Even though it's natural, it doesn't always feel that way.

The ideas in this book can help. You can read them again and again. You can even share them with your friends. Just remember the one secret ingredient that all these tips have in common:

In other words . . .

If you want to **have** friends, you have to **be** a friend. And now you know how!

GLOSSARY

ally: a person who is on your side and helps you when you need it

apologizing: saying that you are sorry

communication: when people exchange ideas and information, often by talking

compliment: something nice you say about someone

conflict: a problem between friends; a disagreement or fight

connecting: making a start to meet and know someone

conversation: talking back and forth

empathy: the ability to understand and share someone else's feelings

fiasco: a spicy sauce (Just kidding! It's something that is a total, messy, embarrassing failure.)

independent: when you're good at thinking and acting for yourself

support: to help and encourage someone; to believe in them

About the Author and Illustrator

Eric Braun is a children's author and editor. He has written dozens of books on many topics, and one of his books was read by an astronaut on the International Space Station for kids on Earth to watch. Eric lives in Minneapolis with his wife, two kids, and a dog who is afraid of cardboard. He does not like sardine smoothies, thank you very much, but he loves being a good friend.

Steve Mark is a freelance illustrator and a part-time puppeteer. He lives in Minnesota and is the father of three and the husband of one. Steve has illustrated many books for children, including *Ease the Tease!* from the Little Laugh & Learn™ series and all the books in the Laugh & Learn® series for older kids.

Other Great Resources from Free Spirit

I'm Like You, You're Like Me
A Book About Understanding and Appreciating Each Other
by Cindy Gainer, illustrated by Miki Sakamoto

For ages 3–8. 48 pp.; PB; full-color; 11¼" x 9¼".

Ease the Tease
by Judy S. Freedman and Mimi P. Black, illustrated by Steve Mark

For ages 6–9. 84 pp.; PB; full-color; 6¼" x 8".

We Can Get Along
A Child's Book of Choices
by Lauren Murphy Payne, MSW, LCSW, illustrated by Melissa Iwai

For ages 3–8. 40 pp.; PB and HC; full-color; 11¼" x 9¼".

Cliques, Phonies & Other Baloney
(Revised & Updated Edition)
by Trevor Romain and Elizabeth Verdick, illustrated by Steve Mark

For ages 8–13. 136 pp.; PB; full-color; 5⅛" x 7".

Join In and Play
by Cheri J. Meiners, M.Ed., illustrated by Meredith Johnson

For ages 4–8. 40 pp.; PB; full-color; 9" x 9"; includes digital content.

The Survival Guide for Making and Being Friends
by James J. Crist, Ph.D.

For ages 8–13. 128 pp.; PB; 2-color; illust.; 6" x 9".

Say Hi When You're Shy
Kids Can Cope Series
by Gill Hasson, illustrated by Sarah Jennings

For ages 6–9. 32 pp.; HC; full-color; 8¼" x 10½".

I Can Learn Social Skills!
Poems About Getting Along, Being a Good Friend, and Growing Up
by Benjamin Farrey-Latz

For ages 5–9. 64 pp; PB; full-color; 8" x 8".

Other Great Resources from Free Spirit

The Weird Series
*by Erin Frankel,
illustrated by
Paula Heaphy*

For ages 5–9. 48 pp.;
PB; full-color;
9½" x 8".

Free Leader's Guide
freespirit.com/leader

Weird!
A Story About Dealing
with Bullying in Schools

Dare!
A Story About Standing
Up to Bullying in Schools

Tough!
A Story About How to
Stop Bullying in Schools

Speak Up and Get Along!
Learn the Mighty Might, Thought
Chop, and More Tools to Make
Friends, Stop Teasing, and Feel
Good About Yourself
(Revised & Updated Edition)
by Scott Cooper

For ages 8–12. 136 pp.;
PB; 2-color; 6" x 9".

Jamie Is Jamie
A Book About Being Yourself
and Playing Your Way
*by Afsaneh Moradian,
illustrated by Maria Bogade*

For ages 4–8. 32 pp.;
HC; full-color; 8" x 8".

**Jayden's Impossible
Garden**
*by Mélina Mangal,
illustrated by Ken Daley*

For ages 4–9. 40 pp;
HC; full-color; 10" x 10".

Free Leader's Guide
freespirit.com/leader

Zach Apologizes
*by William Mulcahy,
illustrated by Darren McKee*

For ages 5–8. 32 pp.;
HC; full-color; 8" x 8".

Interested in purchasing multiple quantities and receiving volume discounts?
Contact edsales@freespirit.com or call 1.800.735.7323 and ask for Education Sales.

Many Free Spirit authors are available for speaking engagements, workshops, and keynotes.
Contact speakers@freespirit.com or call 1.800.735.7323.

For pricing information, to place an order, or to request a free catalog, contact:

**Free Spirit Publishing Inc. • 6325 Sandburg Road, Suite 100 • Minneapolis, MN 55427-3674
toll-free 800.735.7323 • local 612.338.2068 • fax 612.337.5050
help4kids@freespirit.com • freespirit.com**